H · JACOB · JOSEPH · J

PORAH · JOSHUA · RAHAB

ON · HANNAH · SAMUEL · NAOMI

ON · ELIJAH · JOSIAH · DANIEL

HER · NEHEMIAH · ELIZABETH

R · JESUS CHRIST · ANNA

OMAS · The WOMAN at the WELL

OANNA · JOSEPH of ARIMATHEA

THYATIRA · PRISCILLA · EUNICE

NOAH · ABRAHAM · SARAH · REBE

MOSES · MIRIAM · AARON · 2

DEBORAH · JAEL · GIDEON · SAM

RUTH · DAVID · ABIGAIL · SOLO

NAAMAN'S SERVANT GIRL · ES

MARY · JOSEPH the CARPEN

MATTHEW · JOHN · PETER ·

MARTHA · MARY MAGDALENE ·

DORCAS · PAUL · LUKE · LYDIA

Courageous & Bold BIBLE HEROES

50 TRUE STORIES of DARING MEN & WOMEN of GOD

SHIRLEY RAYE
REDMOND

ILLUSTRATIONS BY
Katya Longhi

HARVEST HOUSE PUBLISHERS
EUGENE, OREGON

Published in association with Books & Such Literary Management, 52 Mission Circle, Suite 122, PMB 170, Santa Rosa CA 95409-5370. www.booksandsuch.com

Cover and interior illustrations by Katya Longhi
Cover design, hand-lettering, and interior design by Juicebox Designs

For bulk, special sales, or ministry purchases, please call 1 (800) 547-8979.
Email: Customerservice@hhpbooks.com

Courageous and Bold Bible Heroes

Text copyright © 2022 by Shirley Raye Redmond
Illustrations copyright © 2022 by Harvest House Publishers

Published by Harvest House Publishers
Eugene, Oregon 97408
www.harvesthousepublishers.com

ISBN 978-0-7369-8605-2 (hardcover)

Library of Congress Control Number: 2022931788

Printed in China

22 23 24 25 26 27 28 29 30 / RP / 10 9 8 7 6 5 4 3 2 1

Contents

Introduction

What is courage? According to *Noah Webster's 1828 American Dictionary of the English Language*, courage is "the quality of mind which enables men to encounter danger and difficulties with firmness or without fear or depression of spirits." Sometimes we think courage is exhibited only on the battlefield, that brave people are warriors like Joshua and Gideon. But there are different kinds of bravery.

It takes courage to keep a promise—like Hannah.

It takes courage to remain faithful to God in difficult times—like Daniel.

It takes courage to repent—like Peter.

It takes courage to believe—like Joanna.

And it sometimes takes courage to be kind and generous—like Joseph of Arimathea.

The fifty men and women in this book were brave and faithful. Some were poor. Others were rich. Some survived in difficult times, while others lived in comfort and ease. Some behaved foolishly, while others served the Lord fervently. All of them can help boys and girls learn to love the Lord more intentionally. "We know that in all things God works for the good of those who love him, who have been called according to his purpose" (Romans 8:28).

Noah

Hero of the Flood

The dramatic story of Noah is recorded in the book of Genesis. It is a story of death and destruction. It tells how God rid the world of evil people through a great flood that covered the whole earth. It is also a story of hope and how one righteous man obeyed God by doing just what the Lord told him to do.

Because Noah and his family gained favor in the eyes of the Lord, God gave them building instructions for an ark. This enormous boat was bigger than the SpaceX Starship! Seven pairs of clean animals, such as cows, were taken aboard, along with one pair of all unclean animals, such as mice. When Noah, his wife, their three sons, and their sons' wives were safely aboard, God shut the door of the ark. Then it rained for forty days. The seas rose over the land, and the underground rivers erupted.

When the destruction was over, Noah's family and the rescued animals exited the ark.

A rainbow appeared in the sky at the end of the massive storm. God told Noah this would be a sign that he would never again destroy the earth with a flood. The first thing Noah did after stepping onto dry land was to build an altar to worship the Lord.

God told Noah's family to live in peace, to grow things, and to have many children. Noah is the hero of the flood. All people living today—including you and me—have Noah's DNA in our genes!

NOAH

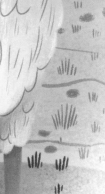

Abraham

The Courage to Trust

Abraham was a wealthy man with abundant livestock, servants, and tents. He lived with his wife Sarah in Ur of the Chaldees. He must have been a rather special man because God reached out to him, making a covenant, or agreement, with him. First, God told Abraham to leave his country, his tribe, and his father's household to go where the Lord led him. God then promised to make Abraham's family a great nation and added, "All peoples on earth will be blessed through you" (Genesis 12:3).

Trusting in the Lord, Abraham did as he was told. Throughout his travels, Abraham marveled how God protected him from powerful kings and warring chieftains. Melchizedek, the important priest-king of Salem, came to Abraham to bless him. When Abraham was nearly one hundred years old, God blessed him and his wife with a son, whom they named Isaac. They were overjoyed. But years later, Abraham's trust was tested once again when God demanded that Abraham sacrifice his beloved son Isaac. Brokenhearted, Abraham agreed. But before he could do so, an angel from the Lord stopped him, providing a ram to be sacrificed instead.

Abraham lived to be a very old man. After his wife Sarah died, he married a woman named Keturah. Together they had six sons. All of God's promises to Abraham came true. He is known around the world as the father of the Jews. Because Abraham trusted God, one of his descendents was born in a Bethlehem stable many years ago—Jesus, the Savior of the world.

Abraham

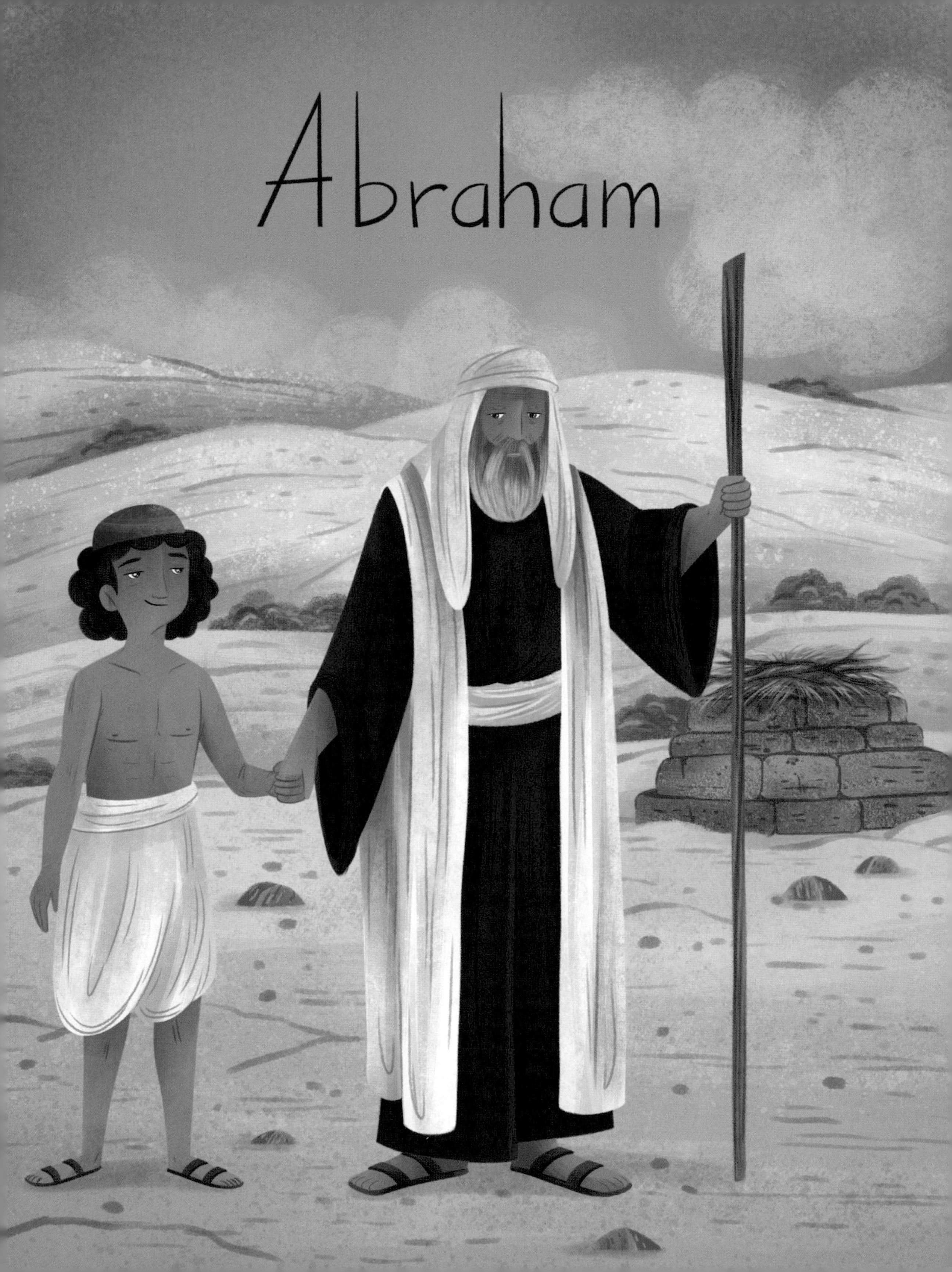

Sarah

Mother of Nations

Sarah was the beautiful wife of Abraham. Because they were wealthy, she stayed busy managing a large household with many servants. She must have been surprised when her husband told her they were moving from their homeland to a place God had directed them to go.

On their travels, they passed through Egypt. Sarah's beauty attracted the attention of the Pharaoh, who took her to his palace. God struck the Pharaoh with a disease until he returned Sarah to Abraham. This happened again when the king of Gerar wanted Sarah for his wife too. Once more, God protected Sarah. He had special plans for her.

Through their long years of marriage, Sarah felt disappointed that she and Abraham didn't have a child of their own. But God had a surprise for them. He told Abraham, "I will bless her, and moreover, I will give you a son by her. I will bless her, and she shall become nations; kings of peoples shall come from her" (Genesis 17:16 ESV).

Sarah laughed when she heard this. She wanted God's words to be true, but she was old—old enough to be a grandmother. Sarah waited. She grew impatient and suggested that Abraham have a child with her young servant, Hagar. But that was not part of God's plan.

At the age of ninety, Sarah gave birth to a baby named Isaac. God's promise came true. Through Sarah and Abraham, all the world has been blessed because Jesus—the Savior and King of kings—was their descendant.

· Sarah ·

Rebekah

The Brave Bride

One evening Rebekah went to the well to draw water. A stranger there changed her life forever. The man's name was Eliezer. He was Abraham's most trusted servant, and Abraham had sent him to find a bride for Abraham's son Isaac. Eliezer had been praying for God's guidance. Before he'd finished praying, Rebekah arrived at the well. She graciously offered him a drink of water and provided water for his thirsty camels. Rebekah even invited Eliezer to spend the night at her parents' home.

Eliezer explained his errand to Rebekah's family. Rebekah willingly agreed to become Isaac's bride. It took courage to leave her family, her home, and her country to marry a man she'd never met. Isaac and Rebekah were happily married for many years before she became pregnant with twins. Rebekah became concerned when she felt the babies struggling within her. "The LORD said to her, 'Two nations are in your womb, and two peoples from within you will be separated; one people will be stronger than the other, and the older will serve the younger'" (Genesis 25:23).

Rebekah always loved Jacob more than his older brother, Esau. She thought Jacob would do a better job leading God's people. She hatched a plan to deceive her husband so that Jacob, not Esau, would receive Isaac's blessing and the family wealth. If only she'd patiently trusted the Lord! As a result of Rebekah's poor decision, Jacob had to flee for his life. He was gone many years, and Rebekah never saw her favorite son again.

Rebekah

Jacob

The Courage to Strive

Jacob is the patriarch, or ancestor, of the twelve tribes of Israel—each tribe is named after one of Jacob's sons. The story of Jacob's life is told in the book of Genesis. Cunning and ambitious, Jacob deceived his father, Isaac, and tricked his twin brother, Esau, out of his birthright. Esau, as the oldest, should have become the head of the family after Isaac passed away. Instead, God's many blessings were given to Jacob.

When Esau threated to kill him, Jacob fled to his mother's relatives in another country.

On the way, Jacob had a dream of a ladder with angels going up and down between heaven and earth. He heard God's voice confirming the promises and blessing made to his grandfather and father, Abraham and Isaac. Grateful for God's assurances, Jacob set up a memorial stone to remember the Lord's goodness.

For many years, Jacob relied on his own cleverness to get what he wanted. As a result, he became a wealthy man with many children, flocks, and servants. When the Lord told him to return to his own land, Jacob prayed for God's protection. Late one night, a divine stranger arrived. Jacob wrestled with him, refusing to let go until he received a blessing from the Lord. As a result of the wrestling match, Jacob was injured and became lame. When the sun rose in the morning, Jacob had a new respect for God and a new name—Israel, which means "he who strives with God."

JACOB

Joseph
The Courage to Forgive

Sometimes it takes courage to forgive those who hurt us. Joseph had many people to forgive. He was the favorite son of his parents, Jacob and Rachel. His eleven older brothers were so jealous of Joseph, they sold him into slavery. They told their grieving father that Joseph had been killed by wild beasts.

In Egypt, Joseph worked for an important man named Potiphar. When Potiphar's wife told cruel lies about Joseph, Joseph was unjustly imprisoned. There he remained true to God and kind to other prisoners. When Joseph correctly interpreted a dream for a fellow prisoner—the royal cupbearer—the grateful man promised to seek Joseph's release.

But the cupbearer forgot his promise until years later when Pharaoh complained about disturbing dreams. Joseph was finally released from prison. He explained that the nightmares were warnings that a famine was coming. Pharaoh put Joseph in charge of building huge warehouses for storing grain. Everything unfolded just as Joseph predicted. There were seven years of abundance followed by seven years of famine. The Egyptians had plenty to eat during the years of famine because Joseph made sure huge amounts of grain were stored up.

Many people came to Egypt to buy food—including Joseph's brothers. They didn't recognize him, but he recognized them. He forgave his brothers for their sin against him and asked them to bring his father, Jacob, and the rest of the family to live comfortably in Egypt.

Joseph was a man with a generous, forgiving spirit. He foretold that Jacob's family would return to their homeland. His prophecy came true many years later when Moses led the people to the Promised Land.

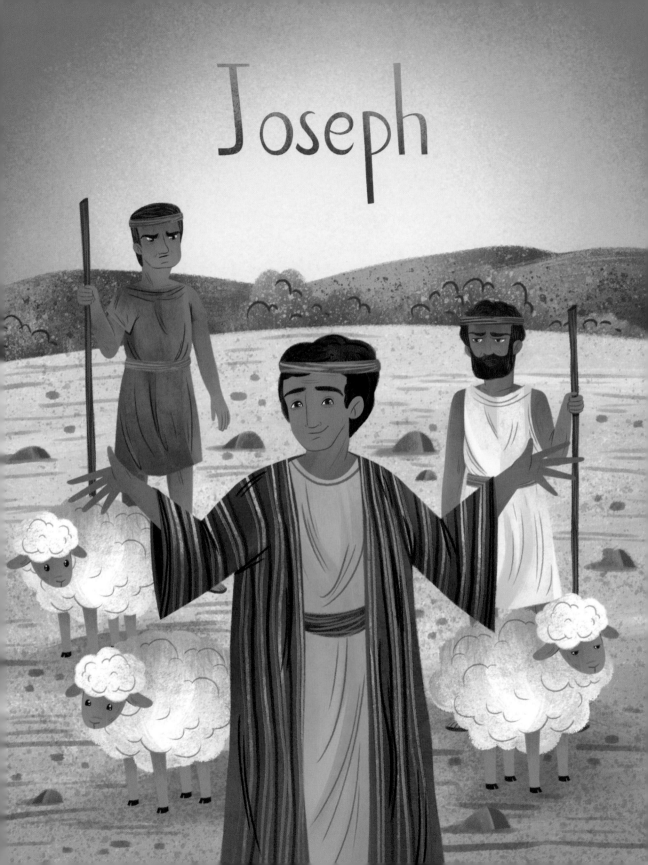

Joseph

Jochebed

The Brave Mother of Moses

Jochebed was born a Hebrew slave in the land of Egypt. Her life was one of hardship and toil. She and her husband, Amram, had a daughter named Miriam, a little boy named Aaron, and a baby named Moses. At that time, the Pharaoh—Egypt's cruel king—feared the growing population of Hebrews in his country. He made a law ordering all newborn Hebrew males be thrown into the Nile River to drown.

But tenderhearted Jochebed refused to cast her sweet baby boy into the crocodile-infested waters. The Pharaoh's law was evil. Jochebed courageously chose to disobey it. At great risk to herself and her family, she hid Moses from the authorities for three months. But soon the wriggling infant became too difficult to hide.

Jochebed made a waterproof basket from water reeds, covering it with pitch and tar. Carefully tucking Moses into the basket, she hid him along the riverbank. Young Miriam secretly kept an eye on the baby from the shore. When the Pharaoh's daughter discovered the baby, she took pity on him. Miriam stepped forward and offered to find a Hebrew woman to nurse the infant. The Egyptian princess agreed. When Jochebed arrived, the Pharaoh's daughter said, "Take this baby and nurse him for me, and I will pay you" (Exodus 2:9).

With heartfelt thanks to God, Jochebed happily took her baby home, not knowing that one day this child, with God's guidance, would lead the Hebrews out of their cruel bondage in Egypt.

Moses

Bold Liberator

Born the son of Hebrew slaves, Moses was rescued from the crocodile-infested waters of the Nile River by the Pharaoh's daughter when he was an infant. Raised and educated as a prince of Egypt, Moses fled after killing an Egyptian guard for beating a Hebrew slave. Moses traveled to Midian, where he worked as a shepherd for forty years.

Speaking through a miraculously burning bush, God commanded Moses to return to Egypt to liberate the Hebrews. Moses protested, insisting he was not a gifted speaker or forceful leader. God assured him that his brother, Aaron, would help. Together, Moses and Aaron boldly entered the palace, demanding that the Pharaoh free the slaves. Pharaoh refused. After enduring ten catastrophic plagues, Pharaoh finally agreed. Later the Pharaoh changed his mind—he needed those slaves to build his royal cities. He ordered the army to bring them back. Moses guided the people to the Red Sea, where God parted the waters so they could walk across on dry land. When the Egyptian army attempted to do the same, the waves rolled over them, and they drowned.

Moses went up to Mount Sinai, where God wrote the Ten Commandments on stone tablets. Returning to camp, Moses discovered his people worshipping a golden calf like the famous bull-god of Egypt. In anger, Moses threw down the stone tablets, which shattered. He offered himself as a sacrifice to pay for the sins of his people, but God spared his life. The great liberator never reached the Promised Land. He died in Moab. To this day no one knows where his grave is.

MOSES

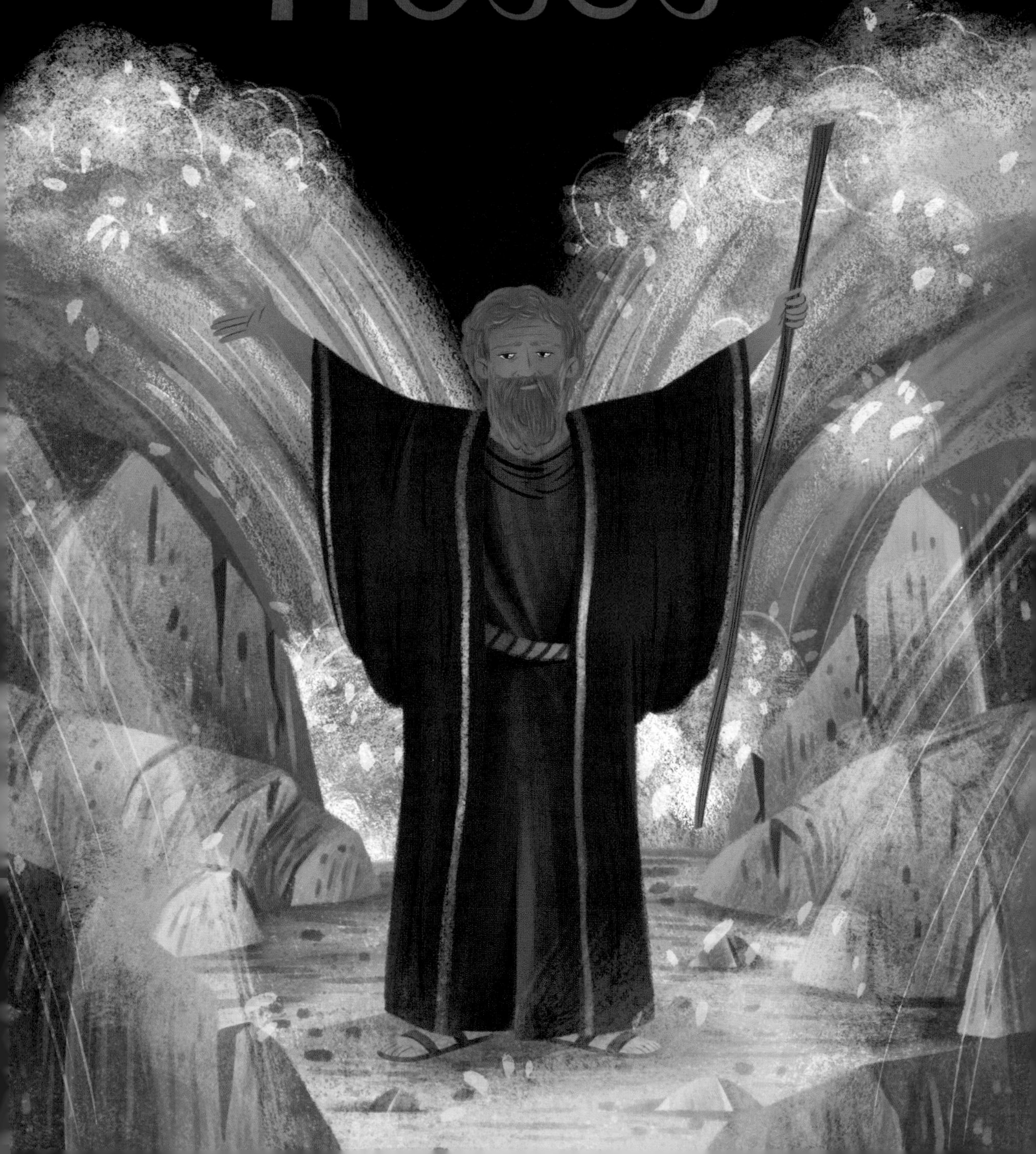

Miriam

The Plucky Sister of Moses

Miriam showed great concern for her baby brother, Moses. She also demonstrated keen wisdom for one so young. When the Pharaoh's daughter rescued Moses from the Nile River and decided to keep him, Miriam boldly stepped forward, offering to find a nurse for the child. The Egyptian princess agreed. Miriam raced home to tell her mother the good news.

Although Miriam didn't grow up with Moses, she encouraged him in his leadership role when God called him to lead the Hebrews out of Egypt. From that time on, she played an important role in the Exodus drama. Miriam witnessed the devastating plagues in Egypt and God's parting of the Red Sea. Following this miracle, Miriam used her tambourine to lead the jubilant Hebrew women in singing praises to the Lord. She was the first woman in the Scriptures to be declared a prophetess (Exodus 15:20).

One day, she criticized Moses and challenged his authority. This angered God. Struck suddenly with leprosy, Miriam was banished from camp for a week. Moses begged the Lord to restore her health. God did so, providing the people with an important lesson in spiritual discipline, repentance, and forgiveness. Years later, Miriam died in Kadesh and was buried there. Hundreds of years after that, the prophet Micah paid tribute to her leadership when he shared these words from the Lord: "I brought you up out of Egypt and redeemed you from the land of slavery. I sent Moses to lead you, also Aaron and Miriam" (Micah 6:4).

Miriam

Aaron

First Hebrew High Priest

Aaron was the first high priest of the Jews. This was such an important religious position that for more than a thousand years, all Jewish priests were descendants of Aaron. He was the son of Amram and Jochebed of the tribe of Levi. He was the brother of Miriam and Moses.

When Moses returned to Egypt after forty years of shepherding Jethro's flocks, Aaron introduced him to the Hebrew elders, convincing them to accept Moses as their leader. Moses and Aaron boldly approached the Pharaoh, demanding that he free the Jews and allow them to leave the country. At God's suggestion, Aaron served as a spokesman for Moses, who often stammered when he spoke.

After enduring ten devastating plagues, the Pharaoh allowed the Hebrews to leave. Aaron and Miriam helped Moses lead the people to the Promised Land. Sometimes Aaron was jealous of his younger brother and made poor choices. When Moses went up to Mount Sinai to receive the Ten Commandments, Aaron gave in to the people's sinful demand for an idol. He constructed a golden calf for them to worship.

During the forty years the people wandered in the wilderness, Aaron married a woman named Elisheba and had four sons. After the tabernacle was built, Aaron began his service as the high priest. He died when he was 123 years old. His priestly garments were passed on to his son Eleazar. Although Aaron made mistakes in his life, he repented and was forgiven.

Aaron

Zipporah
The Bold Wife of Moses

Zipporah was a Midianite girl, the oldest of Jethro's seven daughters. She grew up expecting to marry a man of her tribe. They would raise sheep together and have children. But God had other plans for Zipporah.

One day she and her sisters were watering their father's flocks at the well when rude shepherds harassed them. A man dressed in fine Egyptian clothing came to their rescue. His name was Moses. When the sisters told their father about him, Jethro invited their rescuer to supper. Moses and Jethro became friends. Moses lived with the family for many years, looking after their large flocks. He married Zipporah, and they had two sons—Gershom and Eliezer.

When God ordered Moses to return to Egypt, Zipporah and the boys traveled with him. Zipporah knew that Jehovah God must be obeyed. Like Moses, she and her family were descendants of Abraham—through his son Midian, by his second wife, Keturah. On the journey, Zipporah boldly rescued her husband from God's wrath when Moses neglected to circumcise his sons as required by God's covenant with Abraham.

Before Moses led the Exodus, he sent Zipporah and their sons back to Jethro. Perhaps Zipporah was homesick. Maybe Moses feared that the Pharaoh would kill the Israelites before they could leave Egypt. The couple reunited when Jethro rode out to meet Moses in the desert, bringing Zipporah and the boys with him. "Jethro rejoiced for all the good that the LORD had done to Israel, in delivering them from the Egyptians" (Exodus 18:9 NRSV).

Zipporah

Joshua

Valiant Leader

Courageous in battle. Unfailing in duty. Faithful to God. This was Joshua.

Moses could always count on Joshua during the dramatic Exodus out of Egypt. He was always there when needed. Joshua commanded the defensive efforts when the well-armed Amalekites attacked in the desert. He and his friend Caleb were among twelve spies sent as scouts into Canaan. Joshua and Caleb insisted they could take the land if they remained faithful to God's leading.

Before dying, Moses appointed Joshua to take his place as leader. God blessed Joshua with wisdom and courage. God stopped the waters of the Jordan River from flowing so the people could cross into the Promised Land without boats or bridges. As Joshua prepared to invade the well-fortified city of Jericho, God provided specific directions for the siege. Joshua obeyed, even though the orders seemed foolish by military standards. After seven days of marching around the city walls, the priests blew their rams' horns. Then all the Israelites shouted, and Jericho's walls collapsed.

During a later battle, Joshua commanded the sun to stand still so his warriors could vanquish the enemy before nightfall. The sun obeyed. The Israelites won the battle, just as God promised they would. After conquering Canaan, Joshua used his geography skills to establish boundaries and to divide the land fairly among the twelve tribes. Before he died, Joshua addressed his people, urging them to remain faithful to God and not to worship idols. "Choose this day whom you will serve . . . but as for me and my house, we will serve the LORD" (Joshua 24:15 ESV).

Joshua

Rahab

Bold Rescuer

Rahab was a Canaanite woman who lived in the bustling, fortified city of Jericho. When two of Joshua's spies snuck in, Rahab welcomed them. She explained that everyone in Jericho knew the Lord had parted the Red Sea and helped the Israelites conquer many cities. "As soon as we heard it, our hearts melted, and there was no spirit left in any man because of you, for the Lord your God, he is God in the heavens above and on the earth beneath," she declared (Joshua 2:11 ESV).

Rumors of the spies' presence reached Jericho's king. He sent men to seize them. Rahab acted with surprising courage. After hiding the two Israelites safely on her roof, she told the king's men the spies had left. By lying, she placed her entire household at risk, but Rahab took that chance. It changed her life forever. She helped the spies escape. She knew the Lord would help the Israelites conquer her city. She asked that when the invasion took place, they would spare her life and the lives of her family members.

The spies agreed. Rahab was probably frightened when she heard the trumpet blasts and the battle cries of the invading warriors. Joshua honored the promise his spies had made, and Rahab's household was spared. From that day to this, Rahab has been held in high esteem as a woman of faith and courage.

Rahab later married Salmon of the tribe of Judah and became the mother of Boaz, who married Ruth, the great-grandmother of King David.

Deborah

Judge of Valor

Whenever the L ORD raised up a judge for them, he was with the judge and saved them out of the hands of their enemies as long as the judge lived" (Judges 2:18).

Deborah was one of these judges. She was brave and wise, faithful and true. In Hebrew, her name means "bee." Deborah was indeed busy as a bee sharing God's word, settling disputes, offering spiritual guidance, and ruling over civil matters.

During this time, the people of Israel were terrorized by Jabin, the king of the Canaanites. He had a formidable army and nine hundred iron chariots. Deborah, under God's direction, ordered Barak—a Hebrew warrior—to lead ten thousand Israelites against the foe. Dismayed, Barak knew his soldiers would be outnumbered and ill equipped. He reluctantly agreed to go but only if Deborah accompanied them.

Having total confidence in the Lord, Deborah agreed. She assured the Israelites that the Lord would give them a miraculous victory. She told Barak that the glory of that victory would go to a woman. The battle ended victoriously for the Israelites. Not an enemy was left standing. When Sisera, the enemy's famous general, fled from the battlefield, he was killed by a woman named Jael.

Following the victory, Deborah led her people in praising the Lord. Her song of triumph is one of the longest poems in the Bible. With their enemies vanquished, the people no longer lived in terror. They enjoyed forty years of peace and freedom under bold Deborah's leadership.

Deborah

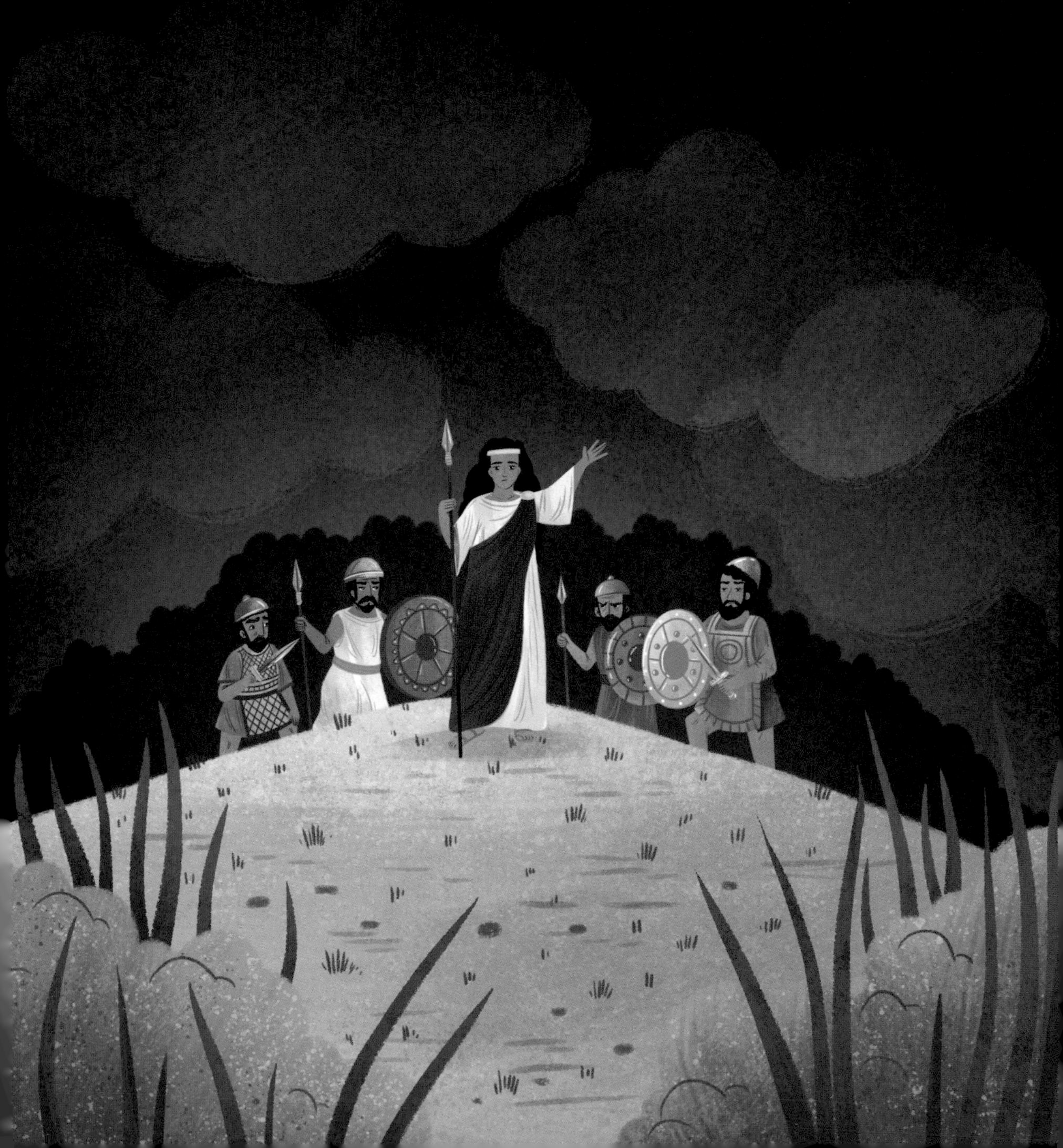

Jael

"Most Blessed of Tent-Dwelling Women"

The story of Jael is one of war, betrayal, and murder. It is a suspenseful account of how the hard-pressed Israelites enjoyed a victory over their enemies with God's divine aid and the help of a woman who was not even a Hebrew.

Jael was the wife of Heber the Kenite, a supporter of Jabin, the Canaanite king. When the Lord led the Israelites to an astounding victory over King Jabin's well-equipped army, General Sisera fled the battlefield in a panic. Looking for a safe place to hide, he made his way to Jael's tent. She invited him inside, offering him lukewarm milk to quench his thirst. Exhausted, Sisera soon fell asleep. Then moving quietly in the tent, Jael collected her hammer and a tent peg—tools she'd been using most of her life. With these she killed the general as he slept. She singlehandedly vanquished the cruel general, who had been brutally oppressing her Israelite neighbors for twenty years.

Jael didn't try to hide what she had done. When Barak, Israel's military leader, arrived in pursuit of Sisera, Jael invited Barak to see for himself that the wicked general was no longer a threat. In that moment Barak realized that Deborah's prophecy had come true, for she had declared the glory of victory would go to a woman. In her song of praise to the Lord, Deborah mentioned Jael, saying, "Most blessed of women be Jael, the wife of Heber the Kenite, most blessed of tent-dwelling women" (Judges 5:24).

Jael

Gideon

The Warrior Who Refused to Be King

In the days of Gideon, the Israelites were vulnerable to attack by enemies who robbed their homes, plundered their cattle, and destroyed their crops. God allowed this calamity because they had been unfaithful by worshipping idols. Finally, God selected a leader to rescue them. When the Lord's angel appeared to Gideon, he was startled by the news that he'd been chosen to lead the people. Gideon asked for proof that this was God's will. The angel instructed Gideon to prepare a food offering. When Gideon did so, the food burst into flames, and the angel vanished.

Gideon obeyed the Lord even though he lacked confidence in his own abilities. When God ordered him to demolish Baal's altar, Gideon did so late at night when no one would see him. He then built a new altar and sacrificed to the Lord. Later, God ordered Gideon to lead the Israelites against their enemies. With thousands of men under his command, Gideon felt confident he could win the battle. Unexpectedly, God ordered Gideon to send most of the men home. With a military force of only three hundred men, Gideon might have felt fearful. Still, he trusted God to do the impossible. That night Gideon led a sneak attack against the enemy army, winning a great victory. The triumphant Israelites wanted to crown him king, but Gideon refused. He didn't desire power and fame.

Under Gideon's leadership, the people enjoyed peace and prosperity for forty years. Even today, believers honor Gideon's faith. The Gideons International is a Bible distribution organization named after him.

Samson

The Strong and Mighty

Hot-tempered. Foolish. Fickle. This describes Samson. He was also fearless when facing the enemies of God's people. Before Samson was born, an angel appeared to his mother, telling her the boy would grow up to deliver Israel from the Philistines' tyranny. Samson was to live a holy life and never cut his hair. God would bless Samson as a leader with amazing strength.

Samson did grow amazingly strong—even killing a lion with his bare hands. However, he let his passions control his behavior. Because of Samson's fierce nature, the Philistines feared him. They continually tried to trap him, but Samson always managed to escape. When Samson fell in love with a Philistine woman named Delilah, she tricked him into revealing the secret of his strength. Delilah had Samson's hair cut while he slept. His enemies bound him with ropes, and Samson couldn't escape because the Lord's power had left him. The Philistines gouged out Samson's eyes and lashed him to a grindstone to work like an ox.

One day the Philistines held a festival for their idol Dagon. Helpless and blind, Samson was led into the temple. Three thousand spectators mocked the once mighty Hebrew hero, but they failed to notice that Samson's hair had grown long again. With humility, Samson asked God to bless him with strength once more. Despite Samson's failings, God answered his prayer. Standing between two pillars, Samson pushed with all his might. The temple collapsed. With his death, Samson killed more enemies of Israel than he'd killed while he was living.

Samson

Hannah
Courage to Keep a Promise

Sometimes it takes courage to keep a promise. Hannah made a promise to God, and she kept it. More than anything in the world, Hannah wanted a baby. She'd been married a long time to Elkanah, who loved her dearly. But God had not blessed them with children. Elkanah had another wife named Peninnah, and together they had several healthy children. Instead of feeling sorry for Hannah, Peninnah cruelly mocked her for being childless. But Hannah never became angry or bitter. Instead, she put her trust in the Lord.

Hannah went to the tabernacle to pray for a son, promising to dedicate the child to God's service. When the priest Eli saw her earnestly praying but not making a sound, he mistakenly assumed she'd been drinking too much wine. He reprimanded her, but Hannah quickly explained she was pouring out her heart to the Lord. Eli then blessed her, asking God to grant her prayer. Returning home more hopeful than before, Hannah soon gave birth to a baby boy. She named him Samuel, which means "God has heard." As soon as Samuel was old enough, Hannah and Elkanah took their toddler to live with Eli. Hannah praised God, thanking him for answering her prayer. Hannah's song is one of the longest praise prayers in the Old Testament.

God blessed Hannah with more children, but she didn't forget Samuel. She visited him each year, bringing him new clothes. Yes, Hannah kept her promise, and her beloved firstborn became a mighty prophet of God.

Samuel
Powerful Prayer Warrior

Samuel was a miracle baby—an answer to his mother Hannah's heartfelt prayer. He was just a small boy when he went to live with the priest Eli at the tabernacle in Shiloh. There he performed easy tasks, such as opening the doors each morning. The Lord spoke directly to Samuel even though he was still a child.

As a judge, priest, and prophet, Samuel served the Lord faithfully through dangerous times. He was a prayer warrior whose intercession on behalf of Israel brought God's blessings to the people. Once while Samuel was sacrificing to the Lord, the Philistines prepared to attack. The fearful Israelites begged Samuel to intercede. Samuel prayed, and the Lord thundered mightily against the enemy. The enemy troops fled. The Israelites pursued them and won the battle. Samuel set up a memorial stone so that everyone would remember the amazing thing God had done that day.

At this time, Israel had no monarchy. The people clamored for a king. They wanted to be like other nations. This distressed Samuel. He urged them instead to pursue a right relationship with the Lord. But God told him to grant the people's request for an earthly king. Obediently, Samuel anointed Saul as Israel's first king. Later, when God grew angry with Saul's disobedience, Samuel secretly anointed a shepherd boy named David to become the next king. Samuel also provided a place of safety for David when Saul tried to have him killed.

When Samuel died, the entire nation mourned the loss of this prayer warrior.

Samuel

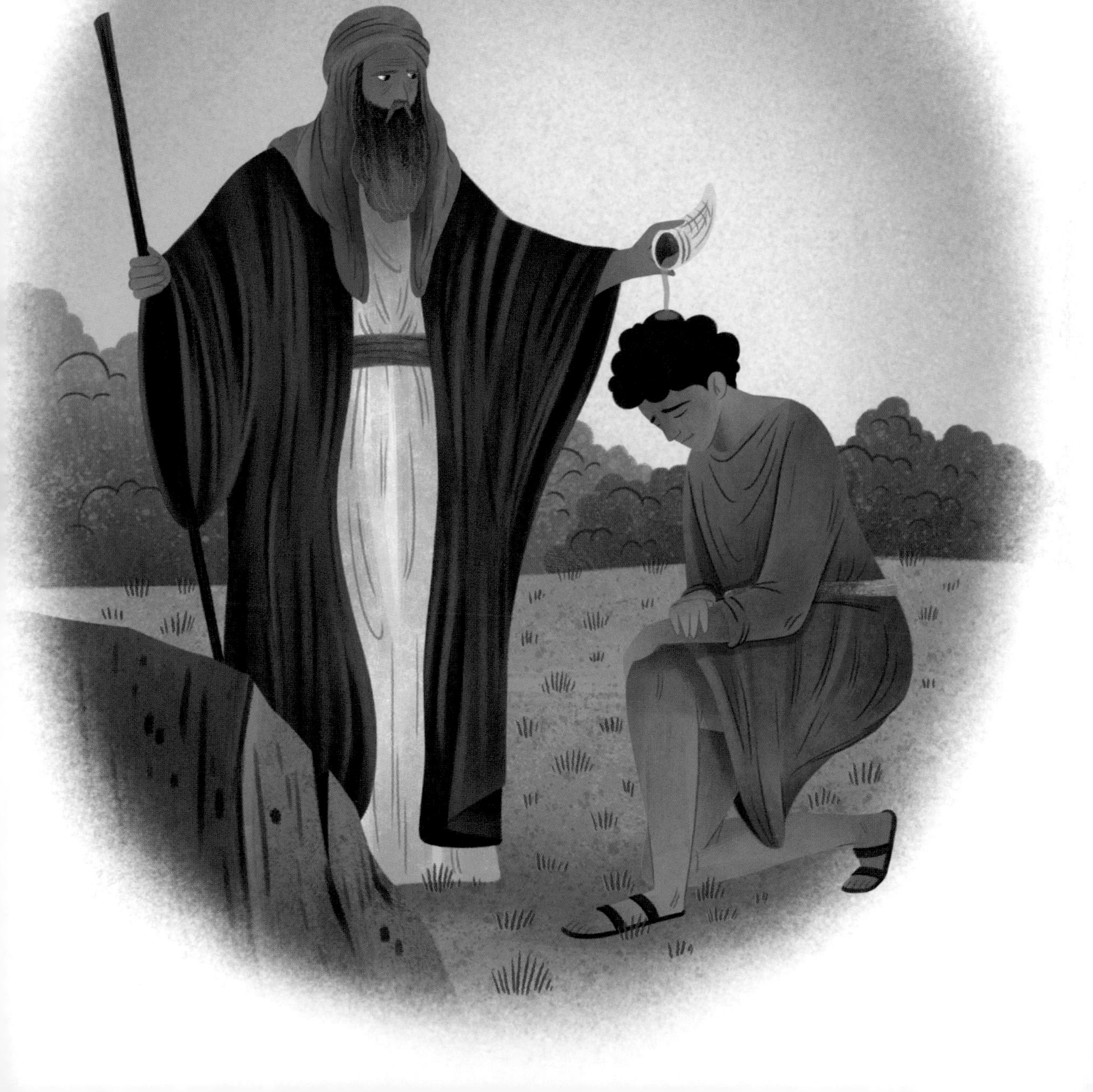

Naomi

Courage in Troubled Times

Naomi was an Israelite woman who lived in Bethlehem. She and her husband, Elimelech, had two sons. When drought and famine struck Judea, they left their homeland in search of a better life. They traveled to Moab, where their sons eventually married Moabite women named Ruth and Orpah.

But tragedy continued to plague Naomi's family. Her husband and then both her sons died, leaving Naomi heartbroken and alone. She owned no property and had no grandchildren to care for her. She urged her sons' young widows to return to their own families. They could remarry one day and have children of their own. Orpah left, but Ruth refused to go. She declared her love for Naomi and the Lord. Touched by Ruth's devotion, Naomi allowed the young woman to accompany her on her journey home to Bethlehem. When Ruth attracted the attention of Boaz, a relative of Naomi's late husband, Naomi served as a matchmaker between them. Soon Boaz and Ruth married and had a baby boy named Obed.

Naomi became a delighted and loving grandmother, giving thanks to the Lord for his blessings. "Then the women said to Naomi, 'Blessed be the LORD, who has not left you this day without a redeemer, and may his name be renowned in Israel! He shall be to you a restorer of life and a nourisher of your old age, for your daughter-in-law who loves you, who is more to you than seven sons, has given birth to him'" (Ruth 4:14-15 ESV).

NAOMI

Ruth

Loving and Loyal

Ruth is one of only two women who have a book of the Bible named after her—and Ruth wasn't even an Israelite! She was born and raised in Moab, a region in modern-day Jordan. She married a Jewish man named Mahlon, the son of Naomi and Elimelech, who'd come to her country to escape a famine in their own land.

Sadly, Mahlon died, along with his father and brother. Ruth was suddenly a young widow, and she mourned her loss. When a grieving Naomi decided to return home to Bethlehem in Judea to be with her relatives, she urged Ruth to return to her own family. But Ruth begged to go with Naomi. "Don't urge me to leave you or to turn back from you. Where you go I will go, and where you stay I will stay. Your people will be my people and your God my God" (Ruth 1:16).

Touched by her devotion, Naomi agreed. Ruth, the young immigrant woman, left her homeland to settle with Naomi in Bethlehem. There she worked hard in the fields each day, gleaning grain. Soon she caught the eye of Boaz, one of the influential men of his community and Naomi's kinsman. Boaz treated Ruth kindly, and he made sure others did too. Following Naomi's guidance, Ruth soon married Boaz. They had a son named Obed, who later had a son named Jesse, who became the father of King David, an ancestor of Jesus the Messiah.

Ruth

David

A Man After God's Own Heart

Musician. Shepherd. Soldier. King.

David was all those things—and more. He was a prayer warrior too. Many of the psalms he wrote are prayers of praise and thanksgiving, prayers of entreaty and confession. The youngest son of Jesse of Bethlehem, David had a heart for God from an early age. He bravely protected his father's flocks, killing both a lion and a bear before they could attack the sheep. While still a teenager, he gained fame when he won a faith-inspired victory against the Philistine enemy, Goliath.

Pleased by David's battlefield success, King Saul invited the young champion to the palace, where Saul enjoyed listening to David's harp playing. David soon became best friends with Saul's son, Jonathan. Then Saul grew jealous and tried to kill David, who spent many years fleeing Saul's wrath. When both Saul and Jonathan were killed in battle, a grieving David wrote heartbreaking psalms about their deaths.

Eventually, David was crowned king of Israel, which became a strong and powerful nation under his leadership. He made Jerusalem the capital city. Although he longed to build a splendid temple for the Lord, David was denied that privilege. However, God revealed the construction plans to him. David shared these with his son Solomon, who succeeded him as king.

Although he made mistakes, David always repented and never worshipped idols. His heart remained true to the Lord. This faithfulness earned him the honor of being called a man after God's own heart (1 Samuel 13:14; Acts 13:22).

DAVID

Abigail

A Bold Peacemaker

Abigail was a peacemaker. She was also wise and beautiful. Her husband, Nabal, was a wealthy man who owned thousands of sheep and goats. Unfortunately, he was also selfish and bad-tempered.

Sheep-shearing time was the busiest of the year. Everyone worked hard. One day, David, who was soon to become king of Israel, sent men to Nabal's ranch to request food. They'd been camped nearby, making sure no bandits or sheep rustlers disturbed Nabal's hired men. Now provisions were low. David and his warriors were hungry. When Nabal rudely denied their request, David angrily vowed to kill every man on the ranch.

When Abigail learned of her husband's unkind refusal to feed David's men, she hastened to prevent bloodshed. She assembled a feast of bread, grapes, meat, and fig cakes—enough to feed an army. She rode out ahead of the supply wagons on her donkey to greet David and his four hundred warriors. Falling to her knees, she begged David for mercy. She prayed for him, blessing him in the name of the Lord. She pleaded with David not to shed innocent blood. David's heart was softened by Abigail's prayerful courage, and he promised not to seek revenge.

Nabal died unexpectedly a few days later. Hearing of his death, David sent a marriage proposal to Abigail. She accepted. After they married, she gave birth to a baby boy name Chileab.

Jesus said, "Blessed are the peacemakers, for they will be called the children of God" (Matthew 5:9). Abigail was blessed.

Solomon

Israel's Wealthiest King

Solomon was still a teenager when he inherited the throne from his father, David. In a dream, God revealed that he would grant Solomon's greatest desire. The young king asked for wisdom and discernment. Pleased, God granted his request. The kingdom of Israel was already well organized and prosperous. Under Solomon's rule, it increased in efficiency, glory, and wealth.

Solomon gained fame for his great intelligence in everything from botany and zoology to military strategy. He also inherited David's creative writing skills. After building the temple, Solomon held a stately dedication service. Fire sizzled down from heaven to consume the massive offerings on the altar.

Foreign leaders came to Solomon seeking advice. The Queen of Sheba arrived with a great caravan of costly gifts including gold, precious stones, and spices. Impressed with the splendor of Solomon's court and awed by his wisdom, she declared, "Praise be to the LORD your God, who has delighted in you and placed you on the throne of Israel. Because of the LORD's eternal love for Israel, he has made you king to maintain justice and righteousness" (1 Kings 10:9).

Despite Solomon's wisdom, he made foolish choices. He married many foreign wives for political reasons, allowing them to build altars to pagan gods. To maintain his expensive palace, he levied high taxes. As Solomon's behavior became more ungodly, the people lost respect for him. During the reign of his son Rehoboam, the kingdom divided, and Solomon's empire was lost.

SOLOMON

Elijah
Bold Prophet

Elijah spent much of his life avoiding capture and death at the hands of evil kings. King Ahab was the worst. He'd married Jezebel, a Phoenician princess, who worshipped the pagan idol Baal. She convinced Ahab to forsake the Lord. Soon it became fashionable for Jews to worship idols and ignore Jehovah God.

Boldly approaching the king, Elijah warned Ahab of God's anger. He explained that the Jews needed to be faithful to the only true God. If they didn't repent, rain would cease for three years. Crops would wither. People and animals would die from hunger. Ahab ignored Elijah. Immediately, it ceased to rain. To escape Ahab's anger, Elijah hid in the wilderness, where the Lord sent ravens to carry food to him. Later, God led Elijah to the home of a widow whose jar never ran out of flour and whose jug never ran out of oil.

One day, Elijah challenged hundreds of Baal worshippers to a contest on Mount Carmel. There Elijah proved that Jehovah is the only true God. Awed, the people asked for forgiveness . . . and then it began to rain. An outraged Queen Jezebel ordered Elijah to be killed. Once again, the faithful prophet fled. And once again, God protected him.

But Elijah was also growing old. God told him to select Elisha as his successor. Elijah did so before he was miraculously carried away into heaven by horse-drawn chariots of fire. Centuries later, Elijah appeared with Jesus and Moses on the Mount of Transfiguration—an amazing event witnessed by a few of the awed disciples.

Elijah

Naaman's Servant Girl
Faithful and Kind

We don't know her name. The Bible doesn't tell us. She's simply referred to as Naaman's servant girl. What we do know is that she was a young Hebrew girl—perhaps twelve years old. She'd been wrenched from her family following a raid on her homeland by Syrian soldiers. She became a servant in the household of Naaman, a Syrian general, who was powerful and proud.

When Naaman was diagnosed with leprosy—a painful and disfiguring skin disease—the girl felt sorry for him. She said to her mistress, "If only my master would see the prophet who is in Samaria! He would cure him of his leprosy" (2 Kings 5:3). She was referring to Elisha.

Naaman's wife told her husband what the girl had said. Naaman sought permission from King Aram to seek out Elisha so he might be cured. But Elisha would not see Naaman personally. He sent a servant with a message that Naaman should dip himself seven times in the Jordan River. Elisha wanted the general to realize that the power of healing comes from God and not the prophet himself.

Naaman was offended. But when his servants begged him to obey, Naaman dipped himself in the river as instructed. Instantly healed, his skin became smooth and pink like a baby's. From that moment, Naaman believed, declaring, "Now I know that there is no God in all the world except in Israel" (2 Kings 5:15).

His young, unnamed servant girl had known that all along.

Naaman's Servant Girl

Josiah
Noble Boy King

Imagine being crowned king of your country at the age of eight. That's what happened to Josiah. He was a child when palace slaves killed his wicked father, Amon. Following Amon's death, Josiah was declared king of Judah. Unlike his father, Josiah wanted to honor the Lord. He purged the land of idols and outlawed child sacrifices. He rid his administration of officials who supported idolatry.

From an early age, Josiah was devoted to obeying God. He longed to restore the kingdom of David and Solomon to its former glory. He collected money from devout Jews to pay for the restoration of the temple, which had been sadly neglected for many years. While repairs were underway, someone discovered a copy of the Torah—the five books of Moses. After reading it, Josiah was ashamed to realize how unfaithful the Jews had been for so many generations. He looked to a female prophet named Huldah for spiritual guidance. She gave him God's blessing, encouraging him to follow God's law.

Eager to do so, Josiah held a national assembly, urging the people to obey God. He led a huge Passover celebration unprecedented in Judah's history and worked diligently to establish godly reforms.

At the age of thirty-nine, Josiah died in battle. The prophet Jeremiah and the rest of the nation of Israel mourned his passing. King Josiah is a good example of how a person is never too young to accomplish important things for the Lord.

Josiah

Daniel

Fearless Faith

When Daniel was a teenager, his country was conquered by Nebuchadnezzar, the powerful Babylonian king. Daniel was taken captive. Imagine how he must have felt knowing he would never see his family and home again. Daniel was taken to Babylon, the capital city of a country now known as Iraq. The ancient Babylonians were noted for their architecture, literature, and astronomy. Daniel and his fellow slaves were educated in these subjects so they could serve the despot king. Despite their circumstances, Daniel and his Hebrew friends remained true to their faith, even their religious laws about diet.

However, they made a dangerous choice when they decided not to worship the king's idols. For disobeying, Shadrach, Meshach, and Abednego were thrown into a fiery furnace. But the Lord saved them. Miraculously, they came out of the furnace unharmed. Not a hair on their heads had been scorched. Daniel also worshipped God even though it was against the law. When he was caught praying, he was thrown into a pit of ravenous lions. God sent an angel to close the lions' mouths, and Daniel survived without harm.

When King Nebuchadnezzar had troublesome dreams, God gave Daniel the ability to explain those dreams to the king. God also blessed Daniel with the gift of visions. These are recorded in the Old Testament book of Daniel. His prophecies about the future of God's people gave the Jews great hope. This steadfast prophet remained faithful even in the worst circumstances.

Esther

The Brave and the Beautiful

Esther's life story is full of drama and suspense. It is the story of how an orphan girl named Hadassah became a queen. She is one of only two women to have a book in the Bible named in her honor.

When the Persian king Xerxes decided to select a new queen, young women from all over the kingdom were rounded up and taken to his palace. They were scrubbed, perfumed, and pampered for a year before being presented to his royal majesty. The king selected Esther because she was the most beautiful. He didn't know she was a Jew. One day the king's prime minister, Haman—an arrogant and vengeful man—convinced Xerxes to slaughter the Jews and confiscate their property. The king carelessly agreed, not realizing his own beloved queen was a Jew.

Guided by her cousin Mordecai, Esther hatched a plan to save their people. Although Esther was fearful, Mordecai encouraged her, saying, "Who knows but that you have come to your royal position for such a time as this?" (Esther 4:14). Esther urged the Jews to fast and pray on her behalf. It was dangerous to approach the king without being summoned. Esther risked death to beg for mercy for her people. Although he could not rescind the law, Xerxes issued a decree stating the Jews could protect themselves. And he ordered Haman to be hanged.

For two days the Jews killed thousands of their enemies in self-defense. Today many Jews commemorate Esther's bravery on the feast day of Purim.

Nehemiah

Ready, Willing, and Able

Nehemiah was a Hebrew captive. He served as a cupbearer for the Persian king Artaxerxes. Nehemiah was not a domestic servant, but a high official with an important position in the palace. Learning of the destruction of Jerusalem, the home of the Jewish people, Nehemiah felt heartbroken. But he was a captive. What could he do? After praying for God's guidance, Nehemiah asked the king for permission to return to Jerusalem to make repairs to the city's wall because without a secure wall, the helpless residents could not protect themselves from invaders. The king trusted Nehemiah and granted him a royal commission to carry out the work, even allowing Nehemiah to obtain wood from the royal forest for the repair of the city gates.

Arriving in Jerusalem, Nehemiah surveyed the destruction with a heavy heart. He met a man named Ezra, who had returned to the city years before with hundreds of Hebrew men, women, and children. They'd tried to rebuild the walls too but were under constant threat from hostile neighbors, such as the Samarians and Ammonites.

Nehemiah was a man of action, ability, and courage. He organized committees. He assigned some men to work on construction and others to arm themselves with swords to fight off attackers. Under Nehemiah's leadership, the wall was repaired in only fifty-two days. Nehemiah and Ezra worked together to restore the city and to instruct the people in following God's laws. With his task complete, Nehemiah dutifully returned to the Persian king to resume his duties in the palace.

Nehemiah

Elizabeth

Mother of John the Baptist

Although righteous in the eyes of the Lord, Elizabeth and her husband, Zechariah, had remained childless throughout their long marriage. One day while Zechariah was performing his priestly duties in the temple, the angel Gabriel delivered news that Elizabeth would give birth to a baby boy. The child was to be named John by divine command. When Zechariah expressed his astonished disbelief, Gabriel took away his ability to speak.

Overjoyed to be pregnant at last, Elizabeth happily welcomed her young cousin Mary, who arrived for a visit. Mary was also expecting a special baby boy. The moment the women greeted each other, Elizabeth felt her baby jump inside her womb. Elizabeth and Mary surely shared their amazing angelic messages with one another. Perhaps they sewed baby clothes together and marveled over the important ministries God had planned for their unborn sons.

Mary stayed with Elizabeth for several months. When Elizabeth's baby was born, the family expected her to name the child after his father. But Elizabeth insisted on the name John. Zechariah wrote "John" on a tablet. In that instant, Zechariah's ability to speak returned.

John grew up to boldly proclaim the coming of Jesus the Messiah. Because of her age, we can assume that Elizabeth died before her godly son was murdered by Herod. How proud Elizabeth would have been had she heard Jesus declare, "Truly I tell you, among those born of women there has not risen anyone greater than John the Baptist" (Matthew 11:11).

Mary

The Mother of Jesus

A young girl living in Nazareth, Mary was engaged to marry a carpenter named Joseph. But before the wedding could take place, an angel named Gabriel told Mary that she was to become the mother of God's one and only Son—Jesus. This incident is known as the Annunciation, which means an announcement took place.

Astonished, Mary humbly accepted the Lord's will, saying, "I am the Lord's servant. May everything you have said about me come true" (Luke 1:38 NLT). When Jesus began to grow inside her, Mary visited her older cousin Elizabeth, who was also expecting a special baby. They rejoiced together. Mary's song of praise to God is one of the most beautiful passages in the New Testament. After baby Jesus was born in Bethlehem, Mary and Joseph fled to Egypt. Joseph had been warned in a dream to take the family to safety because King Herod had ordered the killing of all Jewish baby boys in the area under the age of two. They returned to Nazareth after Herod died.

Mary was with Jesus when he performed his first recorded miracle at a wedding party, turning water into wine. She was also present at his crucifixion. Even in his pain and anguish, Jesus remembered his mother, asking the disciple John to take care of her. She became a part of John's household from that moment on. Following the resurrection, Mary waited faithfully with John and the other disciples for the Holy Spirit to come, as Jesus had promised. Together, they spread the good news of God's salvation.

Mary

Joseph the Carpenter
The Courage to Depend on God

Because he was righteous in the eyes of the Lord, Joseph was chosen to be the earthly father of Jesus. Joseph was a carpenter in the small town of Nazareth in Galilee. He was engaged to be married, but when he discovered that Mary, his bride-to-be, was already pregnant, Joseph was dismayed. He knew the baby could not be his. However, he was a kind man and didn't want to embarrass Mary or cause a scandal. He planned to send her away quietly. But one unforgettable night, an angel appeared to him in a dream, saying, "Joseph, son of David, do not be afraid to take to you Mary your wife, for that which is conceived in her is of the Holy Spirit. And she will bring forth a Son, and you shall call His name JESUS, for He will save His people from their sins" (Matthew 1:20-21 NKJV).

Trusting in the Lord, Joseph obeyed. He took Mary to his home. When it was time to go to Bethlehem to register for the census, they made the journey together. Baby Jesus was born there in a stable because the inn was already filled with other travelers.

It is generally supposed that Joseph died before Jesus began his important ministry. Joseph was a good choice to be a foster father for a little boy. Although he was not rich or powerful, Joseph was kind and honorable—good qualities for a man chosen to care for God's only begotten Son.

Joseph the Carpenter

Jesus Christ

God's Courageous Son

Jesus once said to his disciples, "This is my commandment, that you love one another as I have loved you. Greater love has no one than this, that someone lay down his life for his friends" (John 15:12-13 ESV). Jesus himself was sinless. He never did anything wrong. He never had a bad attitude or evil thoughts. And yet he willingly died on the cross for our sins. This was a loving and courageous thing to do.

Jesus Christ is the fulfillment of the Old Testament promises about the Messiah. Jesus proved he was God's Son by all the miracles he performed. He fed thousands of people with only two dried fish and five loaves of bread. He made crippled people walk again and cured the blind so they could see. He ordered a stormy sea to calm down and could even walk on the waves. He brought dead people back to life! But there were people who hated Jesus. Despite all the evidence, they didn't believe he was God's Son. They planned to have Jesus killed.

But God brought Jesus back to life. After appearing to many people and telling them what he would have them do in his absence, Jesus returned to his heavenly Father. His beloved disciple John wrote a Gospel sharing the good news. "Jesus did many other things as well. If every one of them were written down, I suppose that even the whole world would not have room for the books that would be written" (John 21:25).

JESUS CHRIST

Anna

Enduring Hope

When Anna met Jesus, she was a very, very old woman. She was the daughter of Phanuel of the tribe of Asher. She'd only been a bride for seven short years when, sadly, her husband died, and she became a widow. She may have been poor and probably childless, but Anna did not grow bitter. She found sanctuary in the temple in Jerusalem, where she spent her long life praying, fasting, and faithfully serving God in the Court of the Women.

During her life, Anna experienced personal grief. She also witnessed tragic events, including the bloody conquest of her country by the Roman army. Still, Anna did not despair. She was a woman of hope. One day, a young mother named Mary came to the temple with her infant Son, Jesus, in her arms and her husband, Joseph, by her side. They'd come to dedicate the baby to God and to make a sacrifice of purification as required by Jewish law.

Anna's friend Simeon, a devout man who prayed often in the temple, cradled this special child in his arms, saying a blessing over Jesus. Inspired by God, Anna joined them. "Coming up to them at that very moment, she gave thanks to God and spoke about the child to all who were looking forward to the redemption of Jerusalem" (Luke 2:38).

Anna's faith had been rewarded and her hope justified, for she had lived to see the Messiah—the glory of Israel and the light to the Gentiles.

Anna

Matthew
Salt of the Earth

Imagine being snubbed by your neighbors and having no friends because of your job. That's what life was like for Matthew the tax collector. As a Jew working for the hated Roman government, he was considered a traitor by his own people. One day Jesus walked past Matthew's business booth, saying, "Follow me." On that day Matthew's life changed forever.

He was so thankful to be a part of Jesus's inner circle that he hosted a dinner party in his home so other tax collectors could meet the Messiah and learn about repentance and salvation. This party must have shocked the other disciples. It certainly angered the Pharisees, who believed a rabbi should have nothing to do with such despicable sinners. But Jesus taught his followers an important lesson: that a person's past should be ignored once that person has repented and accepted him as Lord and Savior.

No longer an outsider, Matthew became one of the Lord's most faithful followers. He was probably richer than the other disciples. When Jesus called them the salt of the earth, Matthew knew just how valuable salt was. In his day, it was very expensive. Sometimes Roman soldiers received their wages in salt. Matthew may have accepted salt for tax payments. It was a precious commodity.

Guided by the Holy Spirit, Matthew went on to write a Gospel following the death, burial, and resurrection of his beloved Jesus. His former profession enabled him to keep an orderly and accurate account of Jesus's ministry.

Matthew

John
The Apostle of Love

Before meeting Jesus, John was a follower of John the Baptist, obeying the call to repentance and baptism in preparation for the arrival of the Messiah. When John met Jesus for the first time, the incident made such an impression on the disciple that many years later when John was an old man, he still recalled that the meeting took place at four o'clock in the afternoon.

John was a fisherman by trade with his brother James. The brothers quickly became two of Jesus's closest friends, along with Peter. John and James were nicknamed "sons of thunder" because of their passionate, impetuous personalities. Once when a group of Samaritans refused to allow Jesus to spend the night in their village, John angrily offered to call fire down from heaven to destroy them, but Jesus patiently rebuked him. Before Jesus died, he entrusted his mother, Mary, into John's care.

A prominent leader in the early church, John wrote five books in the New Testament. According to church tradition, he was the only apostle not martyred, or killed for his faith. In fact, John lived to be a very old man. When banished to the Greek island of Patmos, he experienced visions that he recorded in the book of Revelation. Sometimes John is called "the apostle of love" because he wrote about how God so loved the world. He also wrote about the importance of understanding God's truth and our security in Christ's sacrificial love for us.

JOHN

Peter

The Courage to Repent

Simon Peter was a married man who owned a fishing business with his brother Andrew. He was brave, outspoken, and impulsive. He was also humble. Once Jesus told Peter to lower his fishing nets. Peter did so, doubting he would catch anything because he had been fishing all night without anything to show for it. But soon the nets were filled to overflowing. Recognizing a miracle, Peter knelt at Jesus's feet, confessing he was unworthy to be his disciple.

Peter became one of Jesus's closest friends. He saw Jesus perform many other miracles. Even though he was bold, Peter was sometimes fearful too. One stormy night, he courageously stepped out of a boat to walk on the stormy waves toward Jesus. Suddenly overcome by fear, he began to sink. Jesus came to his rescue. On the night that Jesus was taken away to stand trial, Peter was so scared, he denied being Jesus's friend—not once, but three times. Heartbroken by his cowardice, Peter wept bitterly.

Later he repented, changing his behavior. Jesus forgave him. Following the resurrection and Jesus's return to heaven, Peter gave a Spirit-empowered sermon during the festival of Pentecost. Despite many attempts to imprison and kill him, Peter continued to preach the gospel of Jesus Christ and to perform miracles in the Lord's name. Eventually Peter traveled to Rome, where he was put to death during the reign of the cruel emperor Nero. Today followers of Jesus repeat Peter's powerful confession of faith: "You are the Christ, the Son of the living God" (Matthew 16:16 NKJV).

Thomas

Disciple of Courage

Jesus chose Thomas to be one of his twelve handpicked disciples. Jesus gave these men the authority to drive out demons and to heal every disease and sickness. Thomas is sometimes called Didymus, which means "twin," so he probably had a twin brother or sister.

Thomas was a loyal follower of the Lord. He became concerned when Jesus stated his intention of returning to Judea to comfort Lazarus's sisters, who were grieving the death of their brother. The worried disciples reminded Jesus that angry Jews planned to stone him. But Jesus made up his mind to go. That's when courageous Thomas turned to the others and said, "Let us also go, that we may die with him" (John 11:16 ESV).

Many people forget this expression of Thomas's devotion. Instead, they refer to him as "doubting Thomas" because after the brutal crucifixion of Jesus, Thomas didn't accept the testimony of his fellow disciples that Jesus had risen again. Did Thomas really doubt the Lord? Or was he simply overwhelmed by heartbroken feelings? When Jesus later appeared to Thomas, offering to let him touch his wounds, Thomas made a moving declaration of faith: "My Lord and my God!" (John 20:28).

The last mention of Thomas in the Bible is in Acts 1:12-14. He attended a prayer meeting with the other disciples, the faithful women, and Jesus's mother and brothers. According to church tradition, Thomas became a missionary to India. The present-day Christians of Saint Thomas of India claim to be the spiritual descendants of this faithful disciple.

The Woman at the Well

Courage to Share the Good News

One afternoon, Jesus sat down near a well and had a conversation with a woman he met there. We don't know the woman's name, but we do know that she was a Samaritan—a group of people the Jews rejected for ethnic, religious, and political reasons. She was probably a social outcast among her own community because she was drawing water from the well at noon instead of early in the morning with the other women. This special meeting didn't happen by chance—it was planned by God.

While the disciples ventured into town to buy food at the market, Jesus asked the woman for a drink of water. She was astonished that he'd speak to her. She was also curious. As their conversation progressed, the woman asked pointed questions about worshipping God. Most importantly, she grasped the truth of what Jesus shared with her. She told him, "'I know that Messiah' (called Christ) 'is coming. When he comes, he will explain everything to us.' Then Jesus declared, 'I, the one speaking to you—I am he'" (John 4:25-26).

The Samaritan woman immediately believed. Surprised by joy, she returned to the village to tell her neighbors, making her one of the earliest evangelists to share the good news about Jesus Christ. Many of the townspeople came to meet Jesus because of the woman's testimony. They asked Jesus to stay—and he did, for two days. During that time, many came to recognize Jesus as the Savior of the world.

The Woman at the Well

Martha

The Courage to Believe

Martha and her siblings, Mary and Lazarus, were close friends with Jesus. He was occasionally a guest in their home. Martha had a servant's heart. She was a careful hostess, wanting everything to be perfect for Jesus and his companions. She felt comfortable enough to complain to Jesus when her sister, Mary, didn't help with the meal preparations. She boldly expressed her disappointment when Jesus didn't arrive in time to heal her sick brother, Lazarus. But it was for Martha's family that Jesus performed one of his greatest miracles.

Following the death of her brother, Martha learned that Jesus was coming to see her and Mary. She hurried out to meet him, to tell him that had he been there at the time, Lazarus wouldn't have died from his illness. Although grieving, Martha still felt hopeful that Jesus would work a miracle. She knew God would grant Jesus anything he asked for.

Jesus declared emphatically, "I am the resurrection and the life." Then he asked Martha a very important question: "Do you believe this?"

"'Yes, Lord,' she told him. 'I have always believed you are the Messiah, the Son of God, the one who has come into the world from God'" (John 11:25-27 NLT).

This was a remarkable statement for Martha to make, for at that time most people did not believe in resurrection or eternal life—even many Jews did not. Martha had the courage to believe, and Jesus brought her beloved brother back to life again.

Mary Magdalene

A Fearless Follower

Mary Magdalene was from the busy fishing village of Magdala in Galilee, a place occupied by Roman troops and heavily taxed by the Roman government. Mary's life must have been harsh and miserable before she met Jesus, who freed her from the torture of seven demons. With a grateful heart, Mary willingly followed Jesus from that moment on. Jesus treated her and the other women who followed him as beloved sisters. He encouraged them to learn about the kingdom of heaven.

Wherever Jesus went, Mary went too. She financially helped to support his ministry. She wept at the foot of the cross when he was crucified. She accompanied the other grief-stricken women to the tomb to prepare his body with costly oils and spices. When she discovered that he was not there, she wept. Mary thought someone had stolen Jesus's body.

Then she heard someone call her name. Mary turned around. There stood Jesus! Overjoyed, she clung to him and didn't want to let go. Jesus told her to tell the disciples that he was returning to the Father. "Mary Magdalene went to the disciples with the news: 'I have seen the Lord!' And she told them that he had said these things to her" (John 20:18).

Mary had a heart of courage. Her faith was strong. She never abandoned Jesus in those last agonizing hours of his betrayal and death. It seems fitting that she was the first person to see our resurrected Lord.

Joanna

A Woman of Substance

When Jesus healed Joanna, her life changed forever. She became a disciple of Jesus and even said goodbye to her rich husband, her influential friends, and her comfortable lifestyle to travel with Jesus and some of his other followers for a while.

Joanna was the wife of Chuza, the steward for King Herod Antipas. Chuza was a man of some importance at court. He looked after the king's property and managed day-to-day affairs at the palace. Whether Joanna and Chuza were Romans or Jews, we don't know.

Despite her wealth, Joanna was sick. Luke tells us that she was one of several women whom Jesus cured of diseases or evil spirits. From the time of her healing, Joanna followed Jesus from Galilee to Jerusalem, helping to support him with her financial resources. It took courage to walk away from the comforts of her life at court.

Herod had been responsible for the death of John the Baptist, so Joanna must have been frightened when the Pharisees warned Jesus to flee before the king killed him too. But Jesus wasn't afraid of Herod. "He replied, 'Go tell that fox, "I will keep on driving out demons and healing people today and tomorrow, and on the third day I will reach my goal"'" (Luke 13:32).

Joanna joined other women who went to the tomb to anoint Jesus's body with oils and spices following his crucifixion. When an angel announced that Jesus had risen, Joanna and the other women shared the good news. How delighted she must have been knowing her Lord and Savior was alive again!

Joseph of Arimathea
The Courage to Be Kind

Joseph was a righteous man who was seeking God's truth. He was rich and held a powerful position in the Jewish community. A devout Jew from Arimathea, a city northwest of Jerusalem, Joseph was a member of the Sanhedrin. This was a Jewish council or court made up of well-educated rabbis who served as judges over civil and criminal matters pertaining to the Jews.

Joseph also had a secret: He was a follower of the Lord Jesus Christ! However, he kept quiet about his faith because he feared what his fellow members on the council might say or do if they learned that he believed in Jesus as the promised Messiah.

On the night that Jesus was betrayed and arrested, the Sanhedrin met to declare Jesus guilty of blasphemy. They voted to condemn Jesus to death. Joseph refused to take part in the proceedings, and he did not approve of their decision. Following Jesus's cruel death, Joseph boldly approached Pontius Pilate, the Roman governor, to request permission to remove the body from the cross. Pilate said yes to his request. Together with his friend Nicodemus, Joseph wrapped Jesus's body in fine linen. Joseph then respectfully placed the body in his own newly prepared tomb, which had been cut deep into the rock. He securely sealed the tomb by rolling a huge stone over the entrance.

Joseph's secret was a secret no longer, for his loving-kindness in burying Jesus with respect is mentioned in all four of the Gospels.

Joseph of Arimathea

Dorcas

Courage to Serve Others

Dorcas—also called Tabitha—was a follower of the Lord Jesus Christ. She faithfully served him with needle and thread. Dorcas lived in Joppa, a bustling city near modern Tel Aviv. Dorcas was well known for her charity to widows. She was known by both her Aramaic name and a Greek name, so perhaps her ministry included both Jewish and Gentile women.

When Dorcas suddenly died, the Christian community mourned her loss. She'd been loved and respected for her compassion and kindness. The believers didn't know how they could get along without her. Two men were sent to nearby Lydda to fetch Peter. Dorcas may have been dead for two or three days by the time Peter arrived. Her body had been placed in an upstairs room, and the widows gathered there were weeping for sorrow. They showed Peter the robes and other garments Dorcas had sewn—well-made and stylish.

What would they do without her now? Most widows didn't have enough money to take care of themselves, and many had no families to care for them. Peter understood their concern. He sent everyone out of the room, knelt beside the body, and prayed in Jesus's name. At Peter's command, Dorcas came back to life. Then Peter took her back downstairs—alive and well—to her overjoyed friends.

"This became known all over Joppa, and many people believed in the Lord" (Acts 9:42). Today, there are Dorcas Societies all around the world. These organizations carry on her worthy mission to provide clothing for the poor.

Dorcas

Paul

Courageous Missionary

Paul was one of the greatest missionaries of the early Christian church. He wrote more New Testament documents than any other person. He traveled farther and preached the gospel to more people than the other apostles. Also called Saul, he was born in Tarsus, in modern-day Turkey. Paul was a Jewish Pharisee—a strict adherent to the law of Moses. As a young man, he moved to Jerusalem, where he studied to become a rabbi. Paul did all he could to squash the growth of the early church, zealously punishing Christians.

One day, while traveling to Damascus to take Christians as prisoners back to Jerusalem, Paul was suddenly blinded by a bright light, and he heard Jesus speak to him. A Christian named Ananias healed Paul, answered his questions about Jesus, and baptized him. Paul's life was transformed, and he began proclaiming Jesus as the Messiah.

Paul made many missionary journeys, accompanied by friends such as Barnabas and Luke. Paul was frequently flogged and imprisoned. In Caesarea, he was nearly put to death, but because he was a Roman citizen, he was able to appeal to Caesar. Festus, the Roman governor of the province, put Paul on a ship in military custody. On the way, they were shipwrecked. Finally arriving in Rome, Paul was again imprisoned before standing trial.

It is believed that Paul was approximately fifty years old when he was found guilty and beheaded. Before dying, Paul wrote to his friend Timothy, "I have fought the good fight, I have finished the race, I have kept the faith" (2 Timothy 4:7).

Luke

Beloved Physician and Friend

Luke was a doctor, well-educated and cultured. Originally from Antioch, Luke is believed to have been a Gentile, making him the only New Testament writer not born an Israelite. He wrote the longest of the four Gospels as well as the book of Acts—more words than any other New Testament writer. His attention to detail and his careful recording of eyewitness accounts made him a credible historian for the life of Jesus and the early church. Without his careful record, we would not know how the church grew and flourished in the first century following Jesus's resurrection and return to heaven.

With his medical knowledge as well as his compassion for the sick and injured, Luke's writings contain the most healing stories. He probably became acquainted with Mary, the mother of Jesus, who helped him to accurately record the most intimate facts about the Messiah's birth and early life. He also recorded eyewitness accounts from some of the disciples.

Luke was a close friend of Paul's. They made several missionary trips together—making Luke the first Christian medical missionary. Together, Paul and Luke spread the word about Jesus. An enthusiastic believer, Luke used the term "good news" dozens of times in his biblical writings. Toward the end of Paul's life, when he was imprisoned and facing death, his friends and companions deserted him. Luke remained faithful until the end, a fact Paul records simply by saying, "Only Luke is with me" (2 Timothy 4:11).

Today, many hospitals and medical organizations are named for faithful Luke.

Luke

Lydia of Thyatira
Europe's First Christian Convert

Lydia was a successful businesswoman living in the bustling city of Philippi when she first met the apostle Paul and his missionary companions. She was from Thyatira, a thriving commercial city known for its dyeing industry and the production of colored cloth—particularly purple garments, which were expensive and highly prized. Lydia was a dealer in this merchandise. She was probably a wealthy woman with a large home and several servants.

She is referred to as a worshipper of God. This generally means she was a Gentile who had embraced Judaism. She had gathered with other God-fearing women by the river on the Sabbath to pray and worship. There she heard Paul speak about Jesus Christ the Messiah. Moved by the Holy Spirit to accept this truth, Lydia was baptized along with members of her household. She became Paul's first Christian convert in Europe. Sometimes it takes courage to be the first in something.

Although she is mentioned only briefly in the Bible, Lydia provides an important example of Christian hospitality. She was eager to open her home to the traveling missionaries, saying, "If you consider me a believer in the Lord . . . come and stay at my house" (Acts 16:15). Later, Paul and Silas were arrested, flogged, and imprisoned while in Philippi. After being released, they went at once to Lydia's house, where they were no doubt warmly welcomed again with heartfelt thanksgiving to God for their safe return.

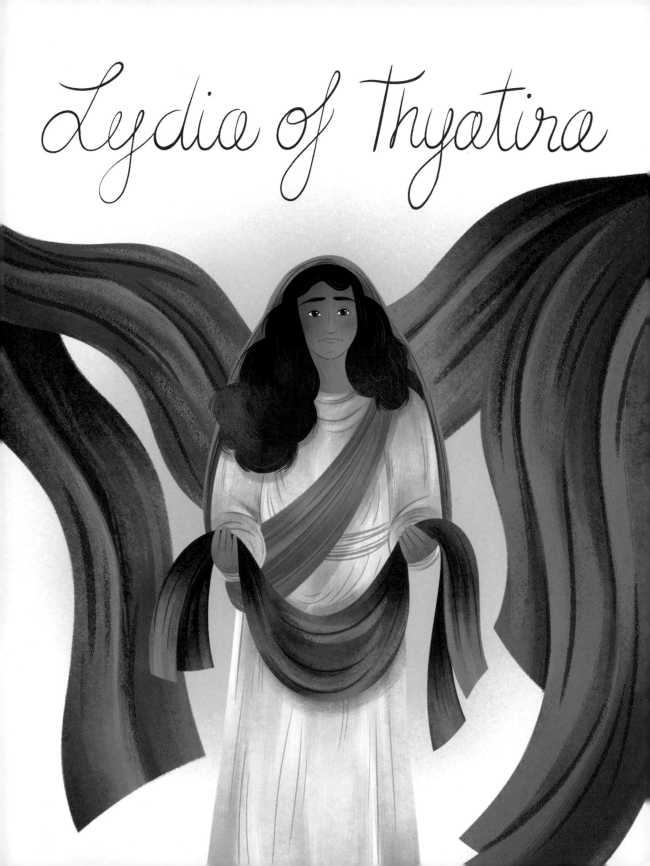

Priscilla

Woman of God's Word

Priscilla was the wife of a Jewish Christian named Aquila. She and her husband had a tentmaking business. Priscilla must have been rather adventurous, because she and Aquila moved often throughout the Mediterranean world. Wherever they went, they opened a home church, teaching the good news of Jesus Christ. Priscilla was kind, hospitable, and hardworking.

It wasn't easy packing up and moving so often. Sometimes they didn't want to go. They moved to Corinth in Greece after being forced to leave Italy when Emperor Claudius banished the Jews. They met Paul in Corinth and formed a lasting friendship. When Paul moved to Ephesus to preach, Priscilla and Aquila traveled with him. They settled down to make tents again and opened another home church.

One day they heard a Jew named Apollos preaching in the synagogue. He was a skillful speaker, familiar with the Old Testament Scriptures. He even mentioned Jesus and the baptism of John. Impressed with the man's boldness, Priscilla invited Apollos to their home so that she and Aquila could explain to him the way of God more accurately.

Eventually, the couple moved back to Rome. Once they settled in, they opened a home church. Because of persecution, it was a scary time to be a Christian, but Priscilla was brave as well as being an effective evangelist. Paul called the couple his fellow workers in Christ Jesus. "They risked their lives for me. Not only I but all the churches of the Gentiles are grateful to them" (Romans 16:4).

Priscilla

Eunice

Passing on a Legacy of Faith

Eunice was the Jewish wife of a Greek man living in Lystra. She and her mother, Lois, were well acquainted with the Old Testament Scriptures. When Eunice gave birth to her son Timothy, she and her mother spent time teaching the boy to read the Scriptures. Perhaps they sat together around a kitchen table, reading a scroll by the light of an olive oil lamp and teaching Timothy about the mighty men of faith, such as Moses, Joshua, and Elijah. They taught him to look forward to the Messiah's coming.

Even though she was a Jewish woman living in a Roman colony where the immoral residents worshipped the Greek deities Zeus and Hermes, Eunice remained committed to the Lord God. Little is known about Eunice's husband. Some suppose he may have died when Timothy was a small child. Eunice, Lois, and Timothy probably converted to Christianity during Paul's first missionary trip to Lystra. His powerful preaching showed them how Jesus Christ fulfilled the Old Testament promises.

Paul was impressed by Eunice and her mother, Lois. He commended them for passing on their heritage of faith to young Timothy, whom Paul came to love as a son. Timothy eventually became Paul's most trusted travel companion and disciple, following him on many dangerous mission trips. When Timothy became a leader at the church in Ephesus, the entire congregation benefitted from his knowledge and faith, which had been instilled in him at an early age by Eunice and her mother, Lois.

Eunice

About the Author

Shirley Raye Redmond is an award-winning writer and newspaper columnist. Her many books include *Courageous World Changers: 50 True Stories of Daring Women of God*, which won a 2021 *Christianity Today* book award. She is also a sought-after workshop speaker and a member of the Society of Children's Book Writers and Illustrators.

About the Artist

Katya Longhi was born in a small town in southern Italy and studied at the Art Academy in Florence and the Nemo NT Academy of Digital Arts. In her spare time, Katya loves to read fairy tales and collect snow globes. She currently works as a freelance illustrator based in Vercelli and has shown her art in numerous exhibitions throughout Italy.

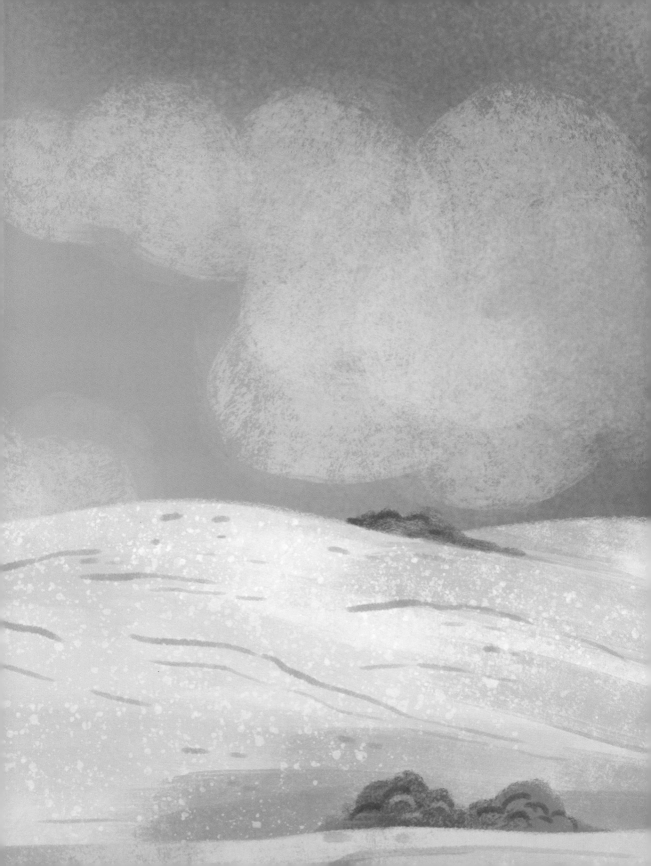

DISCOVER MORE OF GOD'S GREATEST HEROES!

You can learn about more incredible men and women who used their God-given gifts and amazing talents to change history. These real-life superheroes risked it all to save others, stand up for what's right, and spread the good news of Jesus around the world.

HEROES AREN'T BORN – THEY ARE MADE

None of these people started out as courageous world changers or bold defenders, but each one chose to follow God wherever he led them. Guess what? God has awesome plans for you too! All you need to do is say yes to him to begin your life-changing adventure.

Visit CourageousBoldHeroes.com to learn more.

AH · JACOB · JOSEPH · JOCHEBED

PPORAH · JOSHUA · RAHAB

ON · HANNAH · SAMUEL · NAOMI

ON · ELIJAH · JOSIAH · DANIEL

HER · NEHEMIAH · ELIZABETH

ER · JESUS CHRIST · ANNA

OMAS · The WOMAN at the WELL

OANNA · JOSEPH of ARIMATHEA

THYATIRA · PRISCILLA · EUNICE

NOAH · ABRAHAM · SARAH · REBE

MOSES · MIRIAM · AARON · Z

DEBORAH · JAEL · GIDEON · SAM

RUTH · DAVID · ABIGAIL · SOLO

NAAMAN'S SERVANT GIRL · ES

MARY · JOSEPH the CARPEN

MATTHEW · JOHN · PETER ·

MARTHA · MARY MAGDALENE ·

DORCAS · PAUL · LUKE · LYDIA